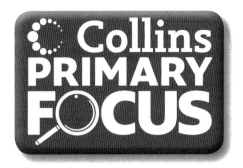

Handwriting

Book 1B

Sue Peet

William Collins' dream of knowledge for all began with the publication of his first book in 1819. A self-educated mill worker, he not only enriched millions of lives, but also founded a flourishing publishing house. Today, staying true to this spirit, Collins books are packed with inspiration, innovation and practical expertise. They place you at the centre of a world of possibility and give you exactly what you need to explore it.

Collins. Freedom to teach.

Published by Collins
An imprint of HarperCollinsPublishers
77–85 Fulham Palace Road
Hammersmith
London
W6 8JB

Browse the complete Collins
Education catalogue at
www.collinseducation.com

Text, design and illustrations © HarperCollins*Publishers* Ltd 2011

Previously published as *Spectrum Handwriting* by Folens Ltd,
first published 2000.

10 9 8 7 6 5 4 3 2
ISBN: 978-0-00-742702-4

British Library Cataloguing in Publication Data
A Catalogue record for this publication is available from the British Library.

Acknowledgements
Fonts from *Handwriting for Windows* used with the permission of KBER.

Every effort has been made to trace copyright holders and to obtain their permission for the use of copyright material. The authors and publishers will gladly receive any information enabling them to rectify any error or omission in subsequent editions.

Design: Mark Walker
Illustrations: Chantal Kees
Cover design: LCD
Cover illustration: Gwyneth Williamson

Printed and bound by Martins the Printers, Berwick-upon-Tweed.

To install the pre-cursive and cursive fonts used in this series, please visit *www.kber.co.uk*, and purchase a licence for *Handwriting for Windows Version 3.0.*

Contents

		Page
Programme overview		**4–5**
Teacher notes		**6–16**
1	Building words: *ab*	**17**
2	Building words: *ack*	**18**
3	Building words: *ad*	**19**
4	Handwriting check 1: Silly sentences *(a)*	**20**
5	Handwriting check 2: "Humpty Dumpty"	**21**
6	Building words: *ag*	**22**
7	Building words: *all*	**23**
8	Building words: *am*	**24**
9	Building words: *amp*	**25**
10	Building words: *an*	**26**
11	Building words: *and*	**27**
12	Building words: *ank*	**28**
13	Building words: *ar*	**29**
14	Handwriting check 3: "Higgledy Piggledy My Black Hen"	**30**
15	Building words: *ash*	**31**
16	Building words: *atch*	**32**
17	Building words: *aw*	**33**
18	Building words: *ay*	**34**
19	Don't forget the punctuation!	**35**
20	Building words: *et*	**36**
21	Building words: *ell*	**37**
22	Building words: *en*	**38**
23	Building words: *est*	**39**
24	Building words: *ick*	**40**

		Page
25	Building words: *iff*	**41**
26	Building words: *ig*	**42**
27	Handwriting check 4: Silly sentences *(e)*	**43**
28	Building words: *in*	**44**
29	Building words: *ing*	**45**
30	Building words: *ip*	**46**
31	Building words: *it*	**47**
32	Handwriting check 5: Silly sentences *(i)*	**48**
33	Building words: *ob*	**49**
34	Building words: *ock*	**50**
35	Building words: *og*	**51**
36	Building words: *op*	**52**
37	Building words: *ot*	**53**
38	Building words: *ub*	**54**
39	Building words: *uck*	**55**
40	Handwriting check 6: "Little Tommy Tucker"	**56**
41	Building words: *ug*	**57**
42	Building words: *um*	**58**
43	Building words: *un*	**59**
44	Building words: *ut*	**60**
45	Handwriting check 7: Silly sentences *(o)*	**61**
46	Handwriting check 8: Silly sentences *(u)*	**62**
47	Handwriting check 9: "The Boy in the Barn"	**63**
	Practice Lines	**64**

Programme overview

Book	Age	Main Content	Main Teaching Aims	Primary National Strategy	Cambridge International Primary Programme
A	Age 4–5 Nursery/Reception/P1 Foundation stage	Pencil control Hand-eye coordination Movements necessary to form letters	To make controlled pencil movements To join two points with a straight or curved line To follow a given sequence of movements	Use a pencil and hold it effectively to form recognisable letters, most of which are correctly formed	
B	Age 4–5 Reception/P1	Pencil control Letter-like movements Recognition of lower case letters linked to upper case letters Upper case letters (alphabetical order) Numbers 0–9	To produce a comfortable pencil grip To produce a controlled line that supports letter formation To write upper case letters using the correct sequence of movements To recognise lower case letters	Use a pencil and hold it effectively to form recognisable letters, most of which are correctly formed	
1A	Age 5–6 Year 1/P2 (Term 1)	Precursive lower case letters, grouped according to movement Recognition of lower case joins Upper and lower case links	To develop a comfortable and efficient pencil grip for forming and linking letters To recognise upper and lower case counterparts To form lower case letters correctly in a script that will be easy to join	Write most letters, correctly formed and orientated, using a comfortable and efficient pencil grip	Develop a comfortable and efficient pencil grip Form letters correctly
1B	Age 5–6 Year 1/P2 (Terms 2 and 3)	Lower case letter formation and joins in a cursive style using common rime patterns Main punctuation marks	To reinforce the link between handwriting, spelling and the recognition of phonic patterns and letter strings To practise correct letter orientation, formation and proportion	Write most letters, correctly formed and orientated, using a comfortable and efficient pencil grip Write with spaces between words accurately	Develop a comfortable and efficient pencil grip Form letters correctly
2	Age 6–7 Year 2/P3	High-frequency word practice Print in the environment Letter joins through common spelling patterns and strings Print for labels, notices etc. School and classroom vocabulary Beginnings of self-assessment	Practice in basic sight vocabulary Reinforcement and practice using the four basic handwriting diagonal and horizontal joins Linking handwriting to phonic and spelling knowledge and patterns Conceptual awareness of space required for printing (for labels, notices etc.)	Write legibly, using upper and lower case letters appropriately within words, and observing correct spacing within and between words Form and use the four basic handwriting joins	Form letters correctly and consistently Practise handwriting patterns and the joining of letters

Scottish Curriculum for Excellence
First stage, Writing (Tools for writing): I can present my writing in a way that will make it legible and attractive for my reader (LIT 1-24a)

National Curriculum for Wales
Foundation Stage objective: develop a legible style of handwriting in order to follow the conventions of written English and Welsh

Revised Northern Ireland Curriculum
Key Stage 1 objective: use a legible style of handwriting

Book	Age	Main Content	Main Teaching Aims	Primary National Strategy	Cambridge International Primary Programme
3	Age 7–8 Year 3/P4	Reinforcement and practice of print and cursive style Copy writing Uses to which handwriting may be put High-frequency word practice Development of spelling patterns	Reinforcement and practice of cursive and printed style to ensure consistency in size and proportion of letters and the spacing between letters and words Purposes and uses of handwriting and print	Write with consistency in the size and proportion of letters and spacing within and between words, using the correct formation of handwriting joins	Ensure consistency in the size and proportion of letters and the spacing of words Practise joining letters in handwriting Build up handwriting speed, fluency and legibility
4	Age 8–9 Year 4/P5	Copy writing Uses to which handwriting may be put High-frequency word practice Development of spelling patterns Development of a personal style Speed writing practice	Reinforcement and practice of cursive and printed style to ensure consistency in size and proportion of letters and the spacing between letters and words Purposes and uses of handwriting and print Consolidation and development of a style that is fast, fluent and legible Presentation, layout and decoration of 'finished' work	Write consistently with neat, legible and joined handwriting	Use joined-up handwriting in all writing
5	Age 9–10 Year 5/P6	Copy writing Development of a personal style Speed writing practice Uses to which handwriting may be put	Purposes and uses of handwriting and print Consolidation and development of a style that is fast, fluent and legible Presentation, layout and decoration of 'finished' work	Adapt handwriting for specific purposes, for example printing, use of italics	Review, revise and edit writing in order to improve it, using IT as appropriate
6	Age 10–11 Year 6/P7	Copy writing Development of a personal style Speed writing practice Uses to which handwriting may be put Links into ICT and fonts	Purposes and uses of handwriting and print Consolidation and development of a style that is fast, fluent and legible Presentation, layout and decoration of 'finished' work	Use different styles of handwriting for different purposes with a range of media, developing a consistent and personal legible style Select from a wide range of ICT programs to present text effectively and communicate information and ideas	Use different genres as models for writing Use IT effectively to prepare and present writing for publication

Scottish Curriculum for Excellence
Second stage, Writing (Tools for writing): I consider the impact that layout and presentation will have and can combine lettering, graphics and other features to engage my reader (LIT 2-24a)

National Curriculum for Wales
Key Stage 2 objective: present writing appropriately (develop legible handwriting; using appropriate features of layout and presentation, including ICT)

Revised Northern Ireland Curriculum
Key Stage 2 objective: develop a swift and legible style of handwriting

Teacher notes

General introduction

Collins Primary Focus: Handwriting is a comprehensive programme designed to support teachers and children through the stages of learning a clear, fluent, legible and fast style of joined writing from the early stages to the top of the Primary phase. The programme provides copiable material that is intended for use through shared sessions, guided group tuition and individual practice.

The programme begins with patterns and movements, which will be necessary to improve hand-eye coordination, fine motor control and individual letter production.

Linked to National Curriculum levels and the Primary National Strategy, the programme encourages a precursive and then a cursive style from the early stages of learning.

The programme aims to link the development of handwriting skills and style to the main patterns and rules of the English spelling system. As children practise the movements necessary to make the joins and patterns of the handwriting scheme, they are also reinforcing the patterns of the main onset, rime and spelling patterns.

By Book 2, children are provided with an opportunity to experiment with alternative letter shapes when forming their own personal handwriting style.

Books 3–6 introduce the notion of keeping a handwriting folder containing samples of material that will prove useful when presenting and setting out work for publication. The books include many uses to which both printing and joined handwriting skills may be put.

Books 3–6 also introduce the concept of two types of handwriting: one style may be used for 'speed' tasks, e.g. personal note-taking; the other, neater, style may be used for presentational work. Self-assessment sheets are included in Book 3 (pp.20 and 63) and Book 6 (p.20). Books 3–6 also link handwriting skills to the basic skills of layout and presentation on a computer keyboard.

The joining of letters in words: which style is most appropriate?

Teachers will always have views about the efficacy or attractiveness of specific letterforms.

It must be remembered that every adult will consider the formation that they use to be the most comfortable to them. However, this does not necessarily make it the most effective formation for children learning for the first time. Teachers must bear in mind the need to develop a handwriting style that is clear, fluent, legible and fast for children learning for the first time.

What about exceptions?

For children with dyspraxia or other handwriting difficulties, the teacher may need to look for SEN support. These children may already be receiving handwriting tuition as part of their support.

Children who move schools may well have already learned another handwriting style. If they enter school during the Infant stage, teachers may wish them to recap pages from the previous book, and this may be completed – with the cooperation of parents – as a homework activity. Children who move schools during the Junior stage may well have formed a personal handwriting style, which, although different, is clear, fluent and legible. It may be inappropriate to alter their handwriting style at this stage.

The notes on particular handwriting difficulties (see p.14 of the Teacher notes in Books 1A–2) may also provide useful information.

Letterforms in the programme

Collins Primary Focus: Handwriting aims for the development of joined handwriting as soon as individual precursive letterforms have been mastered. Specific letterforms have been selected to meet the following criteria:

- They should help children's handwriting to be clear, fluent, legible and fast.
- Each individual lower case letter chosen begins from the main writing line.
- Each lower case letter is taught with both a lead-in and a lead-out stroke. This is to help avoid confusion in young children about whether to

begin a letter at the top or the bottom. It has also proved to be beneficial for children with poor hand control and for dyslexic children.

- The joined lower case letters should, where possible, resemble closely their printed counterparts.
- Letters, such as 's' should have the same form wherever they occur in a word, thus reducing the amount that children need to relearn.
- It is possible to join all lower case letters. One letter ('f') changes from the precursive to the cursive stage. While it is felt that the 'f' used in Book B will be familiar to young children learning to form the precursive letters, the cursive 'f' is used from Book 1A to encourage a more fluent hand.
- The pencil or pen should need to be lifted from the page as little as possible when linking lower case letters in words, thus reinforcing the patterning of joined movements within letter strings as an aid to memorising phonic and spelling patterns.

Precursive Upright (Book B)

A B C D E F G H I J K L M
N O P Q R S T U V W X Y Z
a b c d e f g h i j k l m
n o p q r s t u v w x y z
The quick brown fox jumps
over the lazy dog.

Cursive Upright (Books 1A–1B)

A B C D E F G H I J K L M
N O P Q R S T U V W X Y Z
a b c d e f g h i j k l m
n o p q r s t u v w x y z
The quick brown fox jumps
over the lazy dog.

Cursive Slanted (Books 2–6)

A B C D E F G H I J K L M
N O P Q R S T U V W X Y Z
a b c d e f g h i j k l m
n o p q r s t u v w x y z
The quick brown fox jumps
over the lazy dog.

The following letter styles have been chosen to meet the preceding list of criteria:

Specific letter style options

The reasoning behind each cursive letter style option chosen for use in *Collins Primary Focus: Handwriting* was discussed with several Literacy and SpLD (Dyslexic) practitioners who agreed with the choices.

f	Chosen because, looped from the back, it is easiest to link to all other letters, always joining the same way and thus more fluent.
s	Chosen because it joins in the same way whether it is at the beginning, in the middle or at the end of a word, thus making it fluent and meaning there is less for children to learn.
v	Chosen because it is more legible, most like the printed 'v' and less likely to be confused with the letter 'u'.
w	Chosen because it is more legible, most like the printed 'w' and less likely to be confused with the letter 'u'.
x	This is the only small letter that requires the pencil/pen to be lifted from the paper. This style was chosen because it will join and because it is most like its precursive counterpart. A curved 'x' can often be confused for the letters 'sc'; this is particularly so for dyslexic and less able readers.
y	Chosen because it is more legible, most like the printed 'y' and doesn't involve taking the pencil/pen off the paper.
z	Chosen because it will join and because it is most like its precursive counterpart.

As children move on to join letters in words, they will learn that many letters will join in different places, depending on the letter they are linked to. The programme aims to support the development of strong links between the formation of patterns in handwriting and those involved in phonic and spelling knowledge.

Contents of the programme

Infant Stage

Book A: Foundation Stage and Reception/P1

This book introduces the fine motor movements and pencil control that will be necessary for the formation of letters and patterns. It provides practice in moving from left to right, keeping within 'tramlines' and making the up-and-down and curved movements necessary for letter formation.

Book B: Reception/P1

This book reinforces movements and patterns which will help children to make the movements they will need when learning to form letter shapes. For many children the movements from left to right and from top to bottom may not be intuitive, hence the instruction to 'Start at the ☆.'

Practice is also provided in each of the movements for upper case letters. These have been placed early in the programme because many children will have learned at least some of these letters before they begin formal schooling, and so any inappropriate movements can be corrected early.

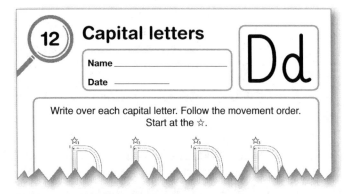

Book 1A: Year 1/P2 (Term 1)

Linked closely to the National Curriculum and Primary National Strategy, this book provides more intense teaching strategies and practice for the first term of formal tuition.

Since it is at this stage that children may learn incorrect or inappropriate movements, each individual letter shape and movement is taught with a lead-in and a lead-out stroke beginning from the writing line. The letters are grouped according to the main movements involved so that children gain extra reinforcement of the shapes and movements involved. By grouping letters according to their movement, it is also hoped to avoid the confusion that many children encounter between letters that may look very similar in print, e.g. 'b' and 'd', 'p' and 'q', 'n' and 'h'.

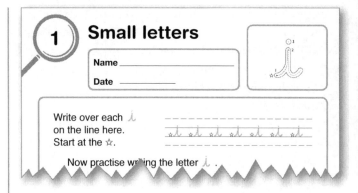

Book 1B: Year 1/P2 (Terms 2 and 3)

To provide extra practice in the transition from precursive to cursive letters, an extra book has been included at this stage. In this book, upper case letters and lower case letters are reinforced through some of the main rime patterns that will be used for spelling. In this way the development of a cursive hand is linked to the introduction of spelling patterns.

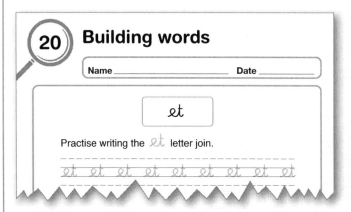

Book 2: Year 2/P3

This book continues the development of linking handwriting to spelling, introducing joins through the main onset groups and blends and the high-frequency words required to be learned and practised by the end of the Infant stage.

Junior Stage

Book 3: Year 3/P4

This book reinforces the handwriting style already learned, through sentences, spelling patterns and simple tongue-twisters and rhymes. During this book, children are encouraged to attempt writing with their eyes closed to help fix the pattern of movements in the mind. (It may be helpful if teachers show children how to place their pencil or pen on the writing line before closing their eyes!)

Through this book, children are introduced to the idea of collating a handwriting folder. Some tasks will need to be completed on another sheet of paper. This book also contains ideas for exemplar material to be retained by children in their handwriting folder.

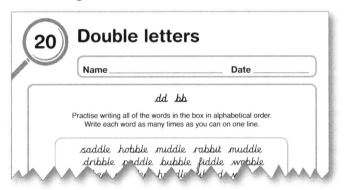

Book 4: Year 4/P5

At this stage, children are encouraged to examine different handwriting purposes and styles. This book also includes settings in which print letters may be appropriate both in upper case and lower case forms.

Links with common spelling rules and patterns and common high and medium-frequency vocabulary are continued. This book also introduces practice in writing at speed.

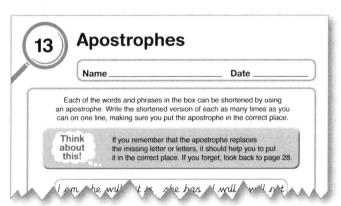

Book 5: Year 5/P6

Throughout this book, children explore different contexts in which a well-formed handwriting style plays an important part. They are asked to use both print and joined styles to transform material from

a range of curricula and everyday situations for presentation to others. By this stage, children will be developing at least three handwriting styles:

- A neat, 'best' form for presentational work that may be produced slowly and with care. This style may be part of a 'school style'.
- A speedier and sometimes less neat form for, e.g. making personal notes or copying work to be presented later. It is perfectly reasonable that some children using this style may begin to 'personalise' their writing. They may begin to add loops or serifs, adopt alternative letterforms and link upper case letters to lower case letters – as many adults do. They may also experiment with a unique signature at the foot of their work. This personalisation should be encouraged as long as it fits the criteria of being clear, fluent, legible and fast.
- A clear, well-formed print style for labels, notices, captions etc. demonstrating judgement about style, size, and spatial awareness of the room available.

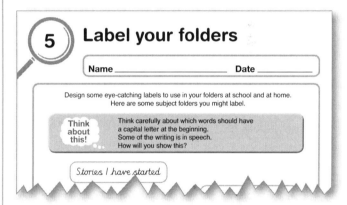

Book 6: Year 6/P7

This book extends children's mastery of the three forms of handwriting listed in the Book 5 entry on this page. Children are encouraged, through a variety of traditional calligraphy and modern presentational tasks, to develop a style that is personal and unique to themselves.
(The relationship between hand-crafted and computer-aided design is extended.)

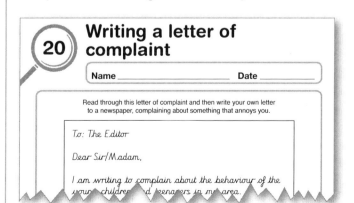

Points to remember when teaching handwriting

Seating

The seating of children for handwriting lessons is particularly important. For this reason, some teachers prefer to specify a 'handwriting table', where the light is particularly good and shines from the side or back of the children.

Many children find it more comfortable to slant their work to the side, away from their writing hand, so that they can clearly see what they are writing. For this reason, they may need more room for handwriting practice than may normally be available.

Left-handed children will need to be seated at the left-hand side of the table or desk. These children might also need a cushion or pad to provide extra height and may often benefit from a sloping surface, which might be provided by using a ring-binder file, on which to rest their paper.

Pencil/pen control

The pencil or pen should be gripped loosely between the first finger and thumb, using the second finger as a rest. The non-writing hand should be used to support and guide the paper. Many children do not learn this automatically, and it may need to be specifically taught.

Children may, even at a very early age, have learned an inappropriate grip. In some cases the hand may curl right over the pencil or pen, making their writing look extremely awkward. Teachers need to make several judgements before intervening to alter such a grip:

- If the child suffers from even a minor manual difficulty, the grip used may be the most comfortable to them.
- If their handwriting is clear, fluent, reasonably legible (to themselves and other children!) and reasonably fast, attempting to change their grip may do more harm than good. These children would benefit from the same practice in patterning and fluency as those with cramped or jerky hand movements. Tips on detecting and correcting difficulties can be found on pp.13–15 of the Teacher notes for Books 3 and 4.
- If altering the grip is the only solution, these children may benefit from recapping of earlier units in the programme as homework practice or in SEN support sessions, to help them relearn the correct movements.

Setting up a special handwriting table makes it easier to make pencil grips or triangular-shaped pencils or pens available for those children who find them more comfortable to use. Several suppliers make triangular-shaped pencils, which children may find more comfortable than a pencil grip.

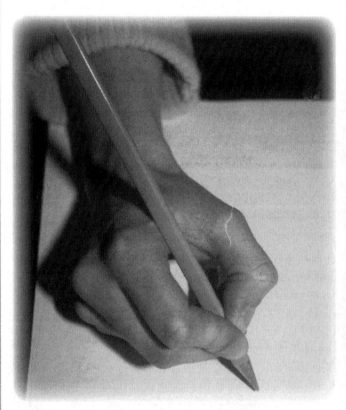

If the layout of the classroom precludes or hinders the setting-up of a handwriting table, children should be taught where their particular handwriting aids are kept and trained to find them for themselves before beginning their Handwriting lesson. Information about these implements and aids should also be made readily available to all staff members.

Pencils and pens

Teachers often feel that providing special handwriting pens for lessons and practice encourages children to take more care with their work. It is now possible to provide a range of rollerball and felt-tip pens that are less likely to leak onto a child's hands or clothes. Many teachers feel that 'biros' are unsuitable because they can easily be smudged, particularly by the left-handed writer whose hand moves across their work.

It is likely, in the main, that children will write in pencil. Teachers may wish to keep some 'special' pencils with other handwriting materials. These pencils should be of reasonable length (left-handers may require a slightly higher grip than their right-handed peers). A range of pencils of differing hardness will also allow children to make judgements about which is the most suitable for them. Pencils should be sharp, but not so sharp that the point breaks on use. Some triangular or wedge-shaped pencils may be included for those who need them. Several suppliers also make triangular-shaped pencils that children may find more comfortable than a grip.

Paper

It is also helpful for children to use different types of paper for writing. A box on the handwriting table might contain paper of different textures, quality, colours and shapes for children to present their sample or test pieces. Preprinted sheets with decorative borders might also be used for display or presentation.

Lined or unlined paper

For Books B–2, teachers may wish each child to have their own handwriting book with staved lines for extra practice. This will also provide additional opportunity to reinforce the onset, rime and spelling patterns plus reinforcement of high-frequency words.

Books 3-6 encourage the use of a handwriting folder for which children may use the copiable pages themselves or separate pieces of paper that are then stored in the folder.

It should be remembered that lines spaced too far apart can be as cumbersome as lines spaced too close together. The final page of Books 1A–6 (p.64) is a set of copiable guidelines. These have been deliberately varied throughout the scheme to provide the optimum type for children with particular handwriting difficulties.

For example:

Books 1A–2

Books 3–6

While many teachers prefer to use unlined paper for everyday work with younger children, *Collins Primary Focus: Handwriting* provides sets of lines (p.64) for practice. As children gain confidence, they may prefer to use a sheet of unlined paper with a set of guidelines placed underneath it.

The writing environment

All of us use both print and joined writing for different purposes. Work in Europe has shown that children are easily able to distinguish between the two if they are used to seeing them. The instructions in the *Collins Primary Focus: Handwriting* books are written in printed script to distinguish them from writing the children will copy. It is helpful if children see signs and posters around the classroom in both printed and joined styles, to help them make judgements about the appropriateness of each for particular situations. As they gain confidence, children will take great pride in producing some of these signs, notices and labels for themselves.

It is also helpful for children to see the upper case and lower case alphabets in the selected letter styles, displayed close to where they write. Children should be encouraged to contribute to the classroom display by copying out class rules, tips for better writing etc. As they learn them, they might also make posters of grammatical definitions, spelling rules or useful proverbs and sayings etc.

If display space permits, examples from children's handwriting may be specially mounted and displayed in the writing area. Where space is at a premium, children might mount 'best' examples of their handwriting in a Big Book anthology.

Before writing

Organisation and timing of lessons

Teachers may use *Collins Primary Focus: Handwriting* as part of a Literacy lesson or as a separate lesson. The programme has been designed for use by a guided group who will then continue on to complete the sheets independent of teacher support. (Children with particular difficulties may work with the support of a teaching assistant.)

Some teachers may prefer to work through particular pages with the whole class before children move into groups to complete the tasks. Pages marked 👥 in the notes on p.16 are considered most suitable for this. Most pages are copiable and have a self-assessment box at the foot of the page that allows the child to decide, in cooperation with the teacher, whether to move on or repeat the task for reinforcement or practice.

Ideally, children should practise their handwriting on a daily basis, and to facilitate this, teachers may decide to work through the content of a particular sheet in a guided group session, once a week, so that children may be observed as they practise in their own Handwriting folders. The children might then complete the sheet independently in the following days.

The handwriting lesson

Handwriting is a motor skill and can be physically quite demanding. Ideally, children should work on their handwriting style by practising it for about 15 minutes every day. If the classroom organisation follows a specified Literacy lesson format, this might be during an independent group activity session.

Where handwriting practice is rotated with other independent activities, children might work independently at other times during the day or at home.

During Books A-2 at least, it is suggested that each new block of skills might be introduced through a shared class lesson. Suggested pages appropriate for this are marked 👥 in the notes on pp.15–16. Teachers may enlarge these worksheets, if they wish, to form the basis of a shared session; or they may prefer to use a whiteboard or blackboard, flip chart or overhead projector to demonstrate the correct movements, joins or the spelling pattern that is being emphasised.

Some children might move from a shared session directly on to working without teacher support. For most children, however, particularly in the early stages, it is suggested that the shared session be followed by a guided group session. During this session, teachers can observe each child to ensure a full understanding of the tasks involved; while children can begin working on each sheet under teacher supervision to ensure correct movement, seating position, pencil grip etc.

Practice and reinforcement

The self-assessment box at the foot of most pages provides an opportunity for children to decide for themselves whether work on a particular sheet needs to be repeated. Teachers might also decide to ask a child to repeat a page during independent work or at home. This will also provide parents or carers with an opportunity to become involved with their children's handwriting development.

The final page in each book provides guidelines and this page can be copied to enable children to practise particular sheets again.

It is suggested that children also have a small handwriting book in which they can practise letters, joins and words that they have worked on during a guided session. The *Collins Primary Focus Word Books* can be used for this purpose.

My First Word Book (age 4-5) 978-0-00-742708-6
My Second Word Book (age 5-6) 978-0-00-742709-3
My Third Word Book (age 6-7) 978-0-00-742710-9
My Fourth Word Book (age 7-9) 978-0-00-743153-3
My Fifth Word Book (age 9-11) 978-0-00-743154-0

Assessment

The principles of good handwriting are that it should be legible, fluent and comfortable to produce at speed. Some children will never be able to achieve the degree of neatness and consistency of others in the class.

The style chosen for these books allows for each letter to be joined to others (with the exception of upper case to lower case), but children should not be penalised, especially after Book 4, for adopting a personal handwriting style in which some letters do not join. What is important is that their personal style of handwriting should be one that meets the principles detailed in the Book 5 entry on p.9.

Children should be encouraged to pay particular attention to handwriting when work is to be presented to others and at the publication stage of a piece of work. For some children, their style will become so much a part of them that they will even use it for rough notes – but few children achieve these heights. *Collins Primary Focus: Handwriting* encourages children, from the start, to make a self-assessment of their work, practising and reinforcing as and when necessary. At the foot of most pages is a 'How did you do?' entry to allow children to make a self-evaluation of their work. Where children regularly work with a partner, the partner may be consulted before the self-evaluation is completed.

Handwriting assessment checklists are provided in Book 3 (pp.20 and 63) and Book 6 (p.20). Teachers and children may use these at any time, to make a more formal assessment.

By storing their work in handwriting folders, children should be able to judge for themselves the progress they are making over a term or year. It should also be possible, through conferences with children, to highlight any periods where handwriting lacks the usual care and attention for whatever reason.

Teachers may also wish to compare work in other subject books with the work within a child's handwriting folder. The different handwriting styles outlined in the entry for Book 5 (see p.9) should be kept in mind when making this comparison.

Handwriting and the use of ICT

Collins Primary Focus: Handwriting, in conjunction with handwriting computer software, aims to link manual handwriting with computer-generated handwriting from the earliest stages. Software may be used to create extra worksheets for practice and reinforcement. Children may also be able to print out their stories, poems and non-fiction writing using handwriting software that features a cursive style.

Detecting and correcting difficulties

How many left-handers are there in your class? Did you know that left-handers often find it difficult to write with a hard pencil? They may grip more tightly and press down harder on the paper. A softer lead pencil may be easier for them to use.

Are all the left-handers in your class able to sit at the left-hand side of a desk for the handwriting session? Are their seats high enough? Are they able to slant and slope their work? Do they use their right hand to steady the paper? Checking these points early can save a great deal of time later remedying poor habits.

Some children with mild dyspraxia may have jerky or shaky hand movements and will never achieve a style of handwriting that looks 'regular'. But they may still achieve a comfortable and legible handwriting style that can be produced at speed.

Many children find triangular-shaped pencils more comfortable to hold and use than a separate pencil grip. Thus it is important to have a range of different writing implements available for the handwriting lesson.

There is a very strong link between handwriting and spelling. People often find that they can write something familiar, e.g. their signature, in a better hand if they write with their eyes closed. When children are memorising a particular spelling pattern, writing the words in a joined hand with their eyes closed may help to fix the pattern in their memory. This may be of particular value to SpLD (dyslexic) children, who need strong reinforcement of the patterns within language.

Just as many people have a special 'telephone voice', so they also often have more than one standard of handwriting. Children should not be expected to achieve the most careful standard for everyday writing. 'Best' handwriting should be considered for use during the publishing stage of writing, particularly if the writing is for presentation to others.

Producing careful handwriting may be physically demanding for many children. In the early stages of learning to join letters, children should be given plenty of time and opportunity to rest their hands. As they become more fluent, short speed tasks in which fluency and legibility take precedence over style may help to prepare them for timed writing tasks or assessment.

NB: More details of activities to correct specific difficulties in handwriting may be found on pp.13–15 of the Teacher notes in Books 3–5.

Book 1B

Year 1/P2 (Terms 2 and 3)

Each join is introduced on its own and then as a rime for different onsets. The pattern is then included in other words where it may occur at the beginning, middle or end. Practice pages on which the patterns taught are included in the context of silly sentences have been inserted at regular intervals. Teachers may wish to use pages from this book to reinforce their work on phonics and spelling in Literacy lessons.

One deliberate feature of this book is the use of patterns that may have more than one sound or may be affected by other letters. For example, 'balloon' has been included with 'all' words (p.23) because it is a) a word that will be familiar to children and b) in producing the word as a joined unit, children are practising the pattern for spelling.

As children master a pattern, they should be encouraged to use it in their other writing.

The patterns 'ing' and 'all' may be two of the first to appear and children should be praised as they transfer knowledge to their other writing books. Many children will still find it helpful to vocalise sounds and patterns as they practise them.

Page 17

Teachers may wish to introduce the format of this book through a class session. The letters are presented in a cursive style, and children may begin to link them as they complete the sheets.

Words are introduced through rime patterns, to help children build a pattern of movements on each page to reinforce the link between handwriting and spelling.

Pages 17–19

Words are introduced first through rime patterns with a single onset and then through a double-letter onset or blend. Children are asked to write only the focused pattern in each case.

As before, teachers should read through each word with children before working on the sheet. Children should then be encouraged to vocalise each pattern as they write and may be able to read the words on completion of the page.

Pages 20, 43, 48, 61–62 (Practice/Samplers)

These pages may be used for diagnostic assessment. The sentences on these pages form silly tongue-twisters that reinforce the focused vowel sounds. Children should be encouraged to recognise which vowel sound occurs most often in each of the tongue-twisters. These tasks may be used to support work in differentiating between vowels and consonants.

Handwriting check 1:
4 Silly sentences

Name _____ Date _____

Write each of these silly sentences in your best handwriting.

Raggedy Maggy drags Barry's fat cat.

The black sack sat on Sally's saddle.

How many times does the letter *a* appear in the two silly sentences?

How many double letters are there in the two silly sentences?

How did you do? Brilliant! OK I need another try.

20   www.collinseducation.com © HarperCollins Publishers Limited 2011

Page 21, 30, 56, 63 (Practice/Samplers)

Throughout this book, children are asked to copy out some rhymes that may be stored in their progress file, displayed in the classroom, or taken home to show to parents or carers.

Teachers may wish to use this task diagnostically to check which children are beginning to join letters within the words and which of the joins may need further practice.

Pages 22–29

In this section, the introduction of rime patterns is augmented by the addition of endings such as 'er', 'ed' and 'le' to create second syllables, and some compound words using the same rime pattern. Teachers might discuss with children what happens to the pattern of the final consonant when these endings are added.

Pages 31–34

This section continues rime patterns around the vowel sound 'a'. Teachers will need to underline the changes that this sound may make as it links with other letters. For example, the sound of 'a' alters when it is linked in different ways: 'ar', 'aw' and 'ay'. By linking the letters, it may support other 'word work' in Literacy lessons on blends, digraphs and phonemes.

Page 35: Don't forget the punctuation! (Practice/Sampler)

This page acts as a reminder for children that upper case letters are important in specific places; for example, at the beginning of each sentence and where proper nouns are used.

This page also reminds children of the need to use correct punctuation when composing and copying sentences.

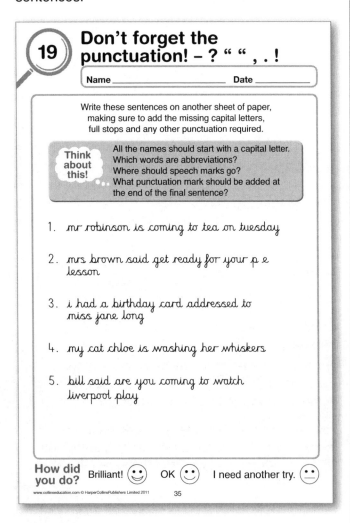

Pages 36–42

This section continues rime patterns around the vowel sounds 'e' and 'i'.

Pages 44–47

Rime patterns with the vowel 'i'.

Pages 49–55

This section continues rime patterns around the vowel sounds 'o' and 'u'.

For the first time while using patterns with 'o', children will learn that letters may join in different ways and at different points. The letter 'o' usually leads out at the top of the letter, ready to join to its successor. Many children will need to practise these particular pages several times. To do so, they may use the guideline page from the back of the book (p.64).

Pages 57–60

This section continues rime patterns around the vowel sound 'u'.

Page 64

A set of guidelines is included for use when teachers wish children to repeat or practise specific task pages on separate sheets of paper.

Teachers may copy the page and children may write directly onto the page, or use it as a guide by placing it underneath a sheet of plain paper.

1 Building words

Name _____ Date _____

ab

Practise writing the *ab* letter join.

ab   ab   ab   ab   ab   ab   ab

Practise writing *ab* on its own.

Join *ab* to these letters to make words.

c   f   t   st

Add *ab* to complete these two words.

st   le   t   let

Choose four words to practise writing again.

How did you do?   Brilliant!   OK   I need another try.

2 Building words

Name _____ Date _____

ack

Practise writing the *ack* letter join.

ack   ack   ack   ack   ack   ack

Practise writing *ack* on its own.

Join *ack* to these letters to make words.

b   h   s   bl

Add *ack* to complete these two words.

t   ing   st   ed

Choose four words to practise writing again.

How did you do?   Brilliant!   OK 😊   I need another try.

18   www.collinseducation.com © HarperCollins*Publishers* Limited 2011

Name _____ **Date** _____

ad

Practise writing the *ad* letter join.

ad ad ad ad ad ad ad

Practise writing *ad* on its own.

Join *ad* to these letters to make words.

d   m   s   gl

Add *ad* to complete these three words.

d   dy   l   le   s   dle

Choose four words to practise writing again.

Handwriting check 1:
Silly sentences

Name _____   **Date** _____

Write each of these silly sentences
in your best handwriting.

Raggedy Maggy drags Barry's fat cat.

The black sack sat on Sally's saddle.

How many times does the letter a appear
in the two silly sentences?

How many double letters are there
in the two silly sentences?

How did
you do?   Brilliant!    OK   I need another try.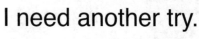

20   www.collinseducation.com © HarperCollins*Publishers* Limited 2011

Handwriting check 2:
"Humpty Dumpty"

Name _____ **Date** _____

Write this well-known rhyme
in your best handwriting.

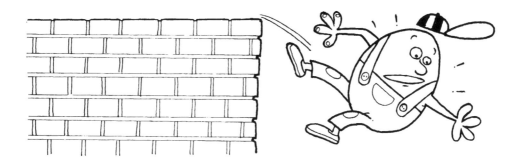

Humpty Dumpty sat on a wall,
Humpty Dumpty had a great fall.
All the King's horses and all the King's men
Couldn't put Humpty together again.

_____
_____
_____
_____
_____
_____
_____
_____
_____
_____

How did you do? Brilliant!   OK   I need another try.

Name _____ Date _____

ag

Practise writing the *ag* letter join.

ag ag ag ag ag ag ag

Practise writing *ag* on its own.

Join *ag* to these letters to make words.

b   *g*   *t*   *fl*

Add *ag* to complete these two words.

h   *gle*   *t*   *ged*

Choose four words to practise writing again.

How did you do? Brilliant!   OK 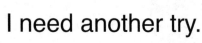   I need another try.

22   www.collinseducation.com © HarperCollins*Publishers* Limited 2011

7 Building words

Name _____ **Date** _____

all

Practise writing the *all* letter join.

all all all all all all all

Practise writing *all* on its own.

Join *all* to these letters to make words.

f   t   b   sh

Add *all* to complete these three words.

b   oon   c   ed   sm   er

Choose four words to practise writing again.

How did you do? Brilliant!  OK   I need another try.

Name _____ Date _____

am

Practise writing the *am* letter join.

am   am   am   am   am   am

Practise writing *am* on its own.

Join *am* to these letters to make words.

h   j   d   st

Add *am* to complete these three words.

sh   e   h   mer   t   e

Choose four words to practise writing again.

How did you do? Brilliant!   OK   I need another try.

24   www.collinseducation.com © HarperCollins*Publishers* Limited 2011

9 **Building words**

Name _____ Date _____

amp

Practise writing the *amp* letter join.

amp amp amp amp amp

Practise writing *amp* on its own.

Join *amp* to these letters to make words.

d   l   d   st

Add *amp* to complete these three words.

d   ed   d   en   h   er

Choose four words to practise writing again.

25

10 Building words

Name _____ Date _____

an

Practise writing the *an* letter join.

an an an an an an an

Practise writing *an* on its own.

Join *an* to these letters to make words.

c   f   b   th

Add *an* to complete these three words.

pl   e   m   ner   t   ned

Choose four words to practise writing again.

How did you do?   Brilliant!   OK   I need another try.

11 Building words

Name _____ **Date** _____

---

and

Practise writing the *and* letter join.

and   and   and   and   and

Practise writing *and* on its own.

Join *and* to these letters to make words.

b   h   s   l

Add *and* to complete these three words.

s   ed   s   y   p   a

Choose four words to practise writing again.

How did you do? Brilliant!    OK   I need another try.

Building words

Name _____ Date _____

| **ank** |

Practise writing the *ank* letter join.

ank   ank   ank   ank   ank

Practise writing *ank* on its own.

Join *ank* to these letters to make words.

b   s   t   sp

Add *ank* to complete these three words.

b   er   pl   s   th   ed

Choose four words to practise writing again.

How did you do? Brilliant!   OK   I need another try.

28   www.collinseducation.com © HarperCollins*Publishers* Limited 2011

13 Building words

ar

Practise writing the *ar* letter join.

ar ar ar ar ar ar ar

Practise writing *ar* on its own.

Join *ar* to these letters to make words.

c f b j

Add *ar* to complete these three words.

e af st

Choose four words to practise writing again.

How did you do? Brilliant!  OK I need another try.

Handwriting check 3:
"Higgledy Piggledy my black hen"

Name _____ Date _____

Write this well-known rhyme
in your best handwriting.

Higgledy Piggledy my black hen,
She lays eggs for gentlemen.
Gentlemen come every day,
To see what my black hen will lay.

How did you do? Brilliant!   OK 😊   I need another try.

www.collinseducation.com © HarperCollins*Publishers* Limited 2011

Building words

Name _____ **Date** _____

---

ash

Practise writing the *ash* letter join.

ash ash ash ash ash

Practise writing *ash* on its own.

Join *ash* to these letters to make words.

b   *d*   *c*   *fl*

Add *ash* to complete these three words.

spl ed   *d ing*   *b ed*

Choose four words to practise writing again.

Building words

Name _____ **Date** _____

| atch |

Practise writing the _atch_ letter join.

atch   atch   atch   atch   atch

Practise writing _atch_ on its own.

Join _atch_ to these letters to make words.

c   l   m   p

Add _atch_ to complete these three words.

c   er th   ed h   ing

Choose four words to practise writing again.

How did you do?   Brilliant!   OK   I need another try.

32   www.collinseducation.com © HarperCollins*Publishers* Limited 2011

17 Building words

Name _____ **Date** _____

aw

Practise writing the *aw* letter join.

aw   aw   aw   aw   aw   aw

Practise writing *aw* on its own.

Join *aw* to these letters to make words.

j   p   s   d

Add *aw* to complete these three words.

s   ing   l   n   th   ed

Choose four words to practise writing again.

Building words

$$ay$$

Practise writing the *ay* letter join.

ay   ay   ay   ay   ay   ay   ay

Practise writing *ay* on its own.

Join *ay* to these letters to make words.

d   p   s   st

Add *ay* to complete these three words.

pl time   d   rel ed

Choose four words to practise writing again.

How did you do?   Brilliant!   OK   I need another try.

   www.collinseducation.com © HarperCollins*Publishers* Limited 2011

19 Don't forget the punctuation! – ? " " , . !

Write these sentences on another sheet of paper,
making sure to add the missing capital letters,
full stops and any other punctuation required.

Think about this! All the names should start with a capital letter.
Which words are abbreviations?
Where should speech marks go?
What punctuation mark should be added at
the end of the final sentence?

1. mr robinson is coming to tea on tuesday

2. mrs brown said get ready for your p e lesson

3. i had a birthday card addressed to miss jane long

4. my cat chloe is washing her whiskers

5. bill said are you coming to watch liverpool play

How did you do? Brilliant!  OK I need another try.

20 Building words

et

Practise writing the *et* letter join.

et   et   et   et   et   et   et   et   et

Practise writing *et* on its own.

Join *et* to these letters to make words.

m   j   s

Add *et* to complete these three words.

l ter   p ted   b ter

Choose four words to practise writing again.

How did you do?   Brilliant!   OK   I need another try.

36   www.collinseducation.com © HarperCollins*Publishers* Limited 2011

Name _____ Date _____

ell

Practise writing the *ell* letter join.

ell ell ell ell ell ell ell

Practise writing *ell* on its own.

Join *ell* to these letters to make words.

b   *f*   *t*   *sh*

Add *ell* to complete these three words.

m   *ow*   *j*   *y*   *s*   *ing*

Choose four words to practise writing again.

How did you do? Brilliant!    OK   I need another try.

22 Building words

en

Practise writing the *en* letter join.

en en en en en en en

Practise writing *en* on its own.

Join *en* to these letters to make words.

h   m   p   t

Add *en* to complete these three words.

g eral   p cil   t th

Choose four words to practise writing again.

How did you do?   Brilliant!    OK   I need another try.

38   www.collinseducation.com © HarperCollins*Publishers* Limited 2011

23 Building words

Name _____ Date _____

est

Practise writing the _est_ letter join.

est est est est est est

Practise writing _est_ on its own.

Join _est_ to these letters to make words.

n   b   z   qu

Add _est_ to complete these three words.

ch   y   j   er   t   ed

Choose four words to practise writing again.

How did you do?   Brilliant!   OK   I need another try.

www.collinseducation.com © HarperCollins*Publishers* Limited 2011   39

Name _____ Date _____

ick

Practise writing the *ick* letter join.

ick ick ick ick ick ick

Practise writing *ick* on its own.

Join *ick* to these letters to make words.

l   s   t   st

Add *ick* to complete these three words.

cl   ed   p   s   t   le

Choose four words to practise writing again.

How did you do? Brilliant!   OK    I need another try.

40   www.collinseducation.com © HarperCollins*Publishers* Limited 2011

Building words

Name _____ Date _____

iff

Practise writing the *iff* letter join.

iff *iff* *iff* *iff* *iff* *iff* *iff*

Practise writing *iff* on its own.

Join *iff* to these letters to make words.

b   m   t   wh

Add *iff* to complete these two words.

cl   s   st   en

Choose four words to practise writing again.

How did you do? Brilliant!   OK   I need another try.

www.collinseducation.com © HarperCollins*Publishers* Limited 2011   41

26 **Building words**

Name _____ Date _____

ig

Practise writing the *ig* letter join.

ig ig ig ig ig ig ig ig

Practise writing *ig* on its own.

Join *ig* to these letters to make words.

b   *d*   *p*   *f*

Add *ig* to complete these three words.

b *gest*   *d* *ger*   *g* *gle*

Choose four words to practise writing again.

How did you do?   Brilliant!   OK    I need another try.

42   www.collinseducation.com © HarperCollins*Publishers* Limited 2011

Handwriting check 4:
Silly sentences

Name _____ Date _____

Write each of these silly sentences
in your best handwriting.

Send ten men to rescue Ken and Debbie.

Three green trees shed their leaves.

How many times does the letter *e* appear
in the two silly sentences?

How many double letters are there
in the two silly sentences?

28 Building words

Name _____ Date _____

in

Practise writing the *in* letter join.

in in in in in in in in

Practise writing *in* on its own.

Join *in* to these letters to make words.

f   p   t   sh

Add *in* to complete these three words.

d ner   t ned   warn g

Choose four words to practise writing again.

How did you do?   Brilliant!   OK    I need another try.

www.collinseducation.com © HarperCollins*Publishers* Limited 2011

Building words

Name _____ Date _____

ing

Practise writing the *ing* letter join.

ing ing ing ing ing ing

Practise writing *ing* on its own.

Join *ing* to these letters to make words.

p   s   z   k

Add *ing* to complete these three words.

k dom   s ing   th s

Choose four words to practise writing again.

How did you do? Brilliant!  OK   I need another try.

www.collinseducation.com © HarperCollins*Publishers* Limited 2011   45

Name _____ Date _____

ip

Practise writing the *ip* letter join.

ip ip ip ip ip ip ip ip

Practise writing *ip* on its own.

Join *ip* to these letters to make words.

d   h   l   wh

Add *ip* to complete these three words.

ch s   sl ped   n per

Choose four words to practise writing again.

How did you do? Brilliant!   OK   I need another try.

46   www.collinseducation.com © HarperCollins*Publishers* Limited 2011

Name _____ Date _____

it

Practise writing the *it* letter join.

it *it* *it* *it* *it* *it* *it* *it* *it*

Practise writing *it* on its own.

Join *it* to these letters to make words.

b   *s*   *p*   *sl*

Add *it* to complete these three words.

b ing   *k* ten   *wh* e

Choose four words to practise writing again.

Handwriting check 5:
Silly sentences

Name _____ Date _____

Write each of these silly sentences
in your best handwriting.

King Griff had a stiff quiff.

_____
_____
_____
_____
_____
_____

King Biff the Bigger giggled and got better.

_____
_____
_____
_____
_____
_____

How many times does the letter *i* appear
in the two silly sentences?

How many double letters are there
in the two silly sentences?

**How did
you do?**   Brilliant!   OK ☺   I need another try.

Building words

33

ob

Practise writing the *ob* letter join.

ob ob ob ob ob ob ob

Practise writing *ob* on its own.

Join *ob* to these letters to make words.

j   m   b   bl

Add *ob* to complete these three words.

b bing   d ber   s bed

Choose four words to practise writing again.

How did you do?   Brilliant!   OK   I need another try.

34 Building words

Name _____ **Date** _____

ock

Practise writing the _ock_ letter join.

ock   ock   ock   ock   ock   ock

Practise writing _ock_ on its own.

Join _ock_ to these letters to make words.

l   d   s   fl

Add _ock_ to complete these three words.

bl __ ed   d __ s   sh __ ed

Choose four words to practise writing again.

How did you do?   Brilliant!   OK    I need another try.

35 Building words

Name _____ **Date** _____

og

Practise writing the *og* letter join.

- -

og   og   og   og   og   og   og

Practise writing *og* on its own.

Join *og* to these letters to make words.

b   c   d   st

Add *og* to complete these three words.

f   gy   j   ged   l   s

Choose four words to practise writing again.

How did you do? Brilliant!   OK   I need another try.

Building words

Name _____ Date _____

op

Practise writing the *op* letter join.

Practise writing *op* on its own.

Join *op* to these letters to make words.

c   h   t   sh

Add *op* to complete these three words.

fl s   st es   st ped

Choose four words to practise writing again.

Building words

Name _____ **Date** _____

_ot_

Practise writing the _ot_ letter join.

_ot   ot   ot   ot   ot   ot   ot   ot_

Practise writing _ot_ on its own.

Join _ot_ to these letters to make words.

_d   h   j   sp_

Add _ot_ to complete these three words.

d ted   l tery   m her

Choose four words to practise writing again.

How did you do?   Brilliant!   OK   I need another try.

www.collinseducation.com © HarperCollins*Publishers* Limited 2011   53

Building words

38

Name _____ Date _____

_ub_

Practise writing the _ub_ letter join.

_ub ub ub ub ub ub ub_

Practise writing _ub_ on its own.

Join _ub_ to these letters to make words.

_c   p   t   st_

Add _ub_ to complete these three words.

cl bed   st by   b ble

Choose four words to practise writing again.

How did you do?   Brilliant!   OK   I need another try.

www.collinseducation.com © HarperCollins*Publishers* Limited 2011

Building words

Name _____ **Date** _____

uck

Practise writing the *uck* letter join.

uck   uck   uck   uck   uck

Practise writing *uck* on its own.

Join *uck* to these letters to make words.

d   m   s   st

Add *uck* to complete these three words.

d   ed   l   y   pl   ed

Choose four words to practise writing again.

Handwriting check 6:
"Little Tommy Tucker"

Name _____ Date _____

Write this well-known rhyme
in your best handwriting.

Little Tommy Tucker,
Sings for his supper.
What shall we get him?
Brown bread and butter!

How did
you do?   Brilliant!   OK 🙂   I need another try.

Building words

Name _____ Date _____

ug

Practise writing the *ug* letter join.

ug   ug   ug   ug   ug   ug   ug

Practise writing *ug* on its own.

Join *ug* to these letters to make words.

b   d   t   th

Add *ug* to complete these three words.

m ger   pl ged   th s

Choose four words to practise writing again.

42 Building words

Name _____ Date _____

um

Practise writing the *um* letter join.

um   um   um   um   um   um

Practise writing *um* on its own.

Join *um* to these letters to make words.

g   h   s   ch

Add *um* to complete these three words.

th   bs   m   my   n   b

Choose four words to practise writing again.

www.collinseducation.com © HarperCollins*Publishers* Limited 2011

Building words

Name _____ Date _____

un

Practise writing the *un* letter join.

un un un un un un

Practise writing *un* on its own.

Join *un* to these letters to make words.

b   n   f   st

Add *un* to complete these three words.

f   ny   g   s   s   shine

Choose four words to practise writing again.

How did you do?   Brilliant! 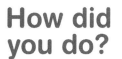   OK   I need another try.

44 Building words

Name _____ Date _____

ut

Practise writing the *ut* letter join.

ut   ut   ut   ut   ut   ut   ut   ut

Practise writing *ut* on its own.

Join *ut* to these letters to make words.

c   h   p   sh

Add *ut* to complete these three words.

b ter   g ter   n ty

Choose four words to practise writing again.

How did you do?   Brilliant!   OK   I need another try.

Handwriting check 7:
Silly sentences

Name _____ Date _____

Write each of these silly sentences
in your best handwriting.

The top cop stopped the rotten robber.

Flopsy mopped the sloppy slops.

How many times does the letter *s* appear
in the two silly sentences?

How many double letters are there
in the two silly sentences?

How did you do?   Brilliant!   OK   I need another try.

Handwriting check 8:
Silly sentences

Name _____ **Date** _____

Write each of these silly sentences
in your best handwriting.

Bugs Bunny has a funny tummy.

- -
_____
- -
_____
- -
_____
- -

The mucky truck missed the lucky duck.

- -
_____
- -
_____
- -
_____
- -

How many times does the letter *u* appear
in the two silly sentences?

How many double letters are there
in the two silly sentences?

How did you do? Brilliant!   OK    I need another try.

www.collinseducation.com © HarperCollins*Publishers* Limited 2011

Handwriting check 9:
"The Boy in the Barn"

Name _____ Date _____

Write this well-known rhyme
in your best handwriting.

A little boy went into a barn
And lay down on some hay.
An owl came out, and flew about,
And the little boy ran away.

_____
_____
_____
_____
_____
_____
_____
_____
_____
_____

How did you do? Brilliant!   OK    I need another try.

How did you do? Brilliant! OK I need another try.